What
The Holy BIBLE Says
about
The Word of GOD

What
The Holy BIBLE Says
about
The Word
of GOD

Fran Rogers

"So shall my word be that goeth forth out of my
mouth: it shall not return unto me void,
but it shall accomplish that which I please,
and it shall prosper in the thing whereto I sent it."
Isaiah 55:11

**What the Holy BIBLE Says about
The Word of GOD**
1st Edition

© 2018 Fran Rogers
Father and Family Books
ISBN-13:978-1732681415

godsgracegodsglory.com

All rights reserved.

Unless otherwise indicated Scripture, quotations are from The Holy Bible, King James Version

Dedication

To those who died as martyrs for their faith rather than betray our Lord who gave His life for our salvation; to those who fought to have The Holy Bible available to all God's people. We praise the Lord our God for His means of preserving His Word for all generations.

Contents

INTRODUCTION
WEEK 1 *Exodus 9 ~ 1 Samuel 15*..........................5
WEEK 2 *1 Samuel 22 ~ 2 Chronicles 36*................11
WEEK 3 *Psalm 12 ~ Psalm 103*..........................17
WEEK 4 *Psalm 105 ~119:80*............................23
WEEK 5 *Psalm 119:81 ~ 168*...........................29
WEEK 6 *Psalms 119:168 ~ Isaiah 28*...................35
WEEK 7 *Isaiah 30 ~ Jeremiah 8*........................41
WEEK 8 *Jeremiah 13 ~ Jeremiah 22*....................47
WEEK 9 *Jeremiah 23 ~ Ezekiel 36*......................55
WEEK 10 *Ezekiel 37 ~ Zechariah 7*..................... 61
WEEK 11 *Zechariah 11 ~ Mark 7*.......................67
WEEK 12 *Mark 16 ~ Luke 4*............................73
WEEK 13 *Luke 8 ~ John 2*..............................79
WEEK 14 *John 4 ~ John 8*..............................85
WEEK 15 *John 10 ~ John 17*............................91
WEEK 16 *Acts 2 ~ Acts 8*...............................97
WEEK 17 *Acts 10 ~ Acts 17*............................103
WEEK 18 *Acts18 ~ Romans 8*..........................109
WEEK 19 *Romans 15 ~ Galatians 5*..................... 115
WEEK 20 *Galatians 6 ~ Colossians 1*....................121
WEEK 21 *Colossians 3 ~ 1 Timothy 3*..................127
WEEK 22 *2 Timothy 2 ~ Hebrews 4*....................133
WEEK 23 *Hebrew 5 ~ Hebrew 13*......................141
WEEK 24 *James 1 ~ 2 Peter 3*..........................149
WEEK 25 *1 John 1 ~ Revelation 5*......................159
WEEK 26 *Revelation 11 ~ Revelation 20*................169
ABOUT THE AUTHOR..........................175

INTRODUCTION

This second book in the series, *What the Holy Bible Says about The Word of GOD* is much longer than the first book. Ten weeks would not be sufficient for God to explain what He wants to say about Himself. The same power of His light in our hearts is the same power that proceeds from His written Word and through His living Word, Jesus Christ. His Word informs, reforms, transforms, and conforms us to the image of Christ, (*The Garden of God's Word*) restoring the image of God that was lost to us in the Garden of Eden.

This twenty-six-week devotional study begins slowly and builds throughout the pages of His Word to a height of joy and excitement during our study. When we come to the end, we can rejoice that we have mined His Word and come away with the treasures that are hidden there.

The same method applies to this study as with the first one. The time you spend meditating on what you find will determine the love and joy you receive from it. It is a simple study, requiring time in prayer with our Lord and the leading of His Holy Spirit.

Using *Strong's Concordance* for the King James Version, we have listed the references for daily study and meditation, with a review and evaluation at the end of each week. You may find it helpful to use another version in addition to the KJV; perhaps the New King James or American Standard Version.

Along with this and other studies we recommend *The Garden of GOD'S WORD ~ The Purpose and Delight of BIBLE STUDY*, second of the series *Little Books About the Magnitude of God*.

Fran Rogers   2018

WEEK 1
Exodus 9 ~ 1 Samuel 15

DAY 1

READ Exodus 9:13-35

"He that feared the word of the Lord among the servants of Pharaoh made his servants and his cattle flee into the houses;
And he that regarded not the word of the Lord left his servants and his cattle in the field." Vs. 20-21

What does the power of God's Word do? Vs. 29,30

On a scale of 1 to 10 how important has the Word of God ~ the word of the Lord" ~ been in your life? Have you feared the word of the Lord or despised it? Let this question be uppermost in your thoughts as you continue in this study. Compare at the end.
Pray for the fear of His Word in your heart and life.

DAY 2

READ Numbers 15:22-36

"Because he hath despised the word of the LORD, and hath broken his commandment, that soul shall utterly be cut off; his iniquity shall be upon him." Vs. 31

What is the result of despising God's word?

Pray that the Lord give you a deeper desire for His Word.

🕮 DAY 3

READ Deuteronomy 8:1-20

"And he humbled thee, and suffered thee to hunger, and fed thee with manna, which thou knewest not, neither did thy fathers know; that he might make thee know that man doth not live by bread only, but by every word that proceedeth out of the mouth of the LORD doth man live." Vs. 3

What are the children of God told to remember (not to forget)? Vs. 2, 5, 11, 14, 18, 19, 20

Pray that you remember what God's Word says.

🕮 DAY 4

READ Deuteronomy 30:1-20

"But the word is very nigh unto thee, in thy mouth, and in thy heart, that thou mayest do it." Vs. 14

Where does God's word work in us? Vs. 2, 6, 10, 14

What does it work in us? 6, 8

Pray for God's love and obedience in your heart.

❧ DAY 5

READ Deuteronomy 33:1-9

"Yea, he loved the people; all his saints are in thy hand: and they sat down at thy feet; everyone shall receive of thy words." Vs. 3

"Who said unto his father and to his mother, I have not seen him; neither did he acknowledge his brethren, nor knew his own children: for they have observed thy word and kept thy covenant." Vs. 3, 9

To what is God's word referred?
Vs. 2
Vs. 4
Vs. 9
Pray to understand what God's covenant blessings are.

❧ DAY 6

READ Deuteronomy 33:26-34:7

"So Moses the servant of the LORD died there in the land of Moab, according to the word of the LORD." Vs.5

What do we see of God in these verses?

Pray that you will know God as your refuge and shield.

DAY 7

READ 1 Samuel 15:1-24

"For rebellion is as the sin of witchcraft, and stubbornness is as iniquity and idolatry. Because thou hast rejected the word of the LORD, he hath also rejected thee from being king." Vs. 23

How does God see our disobedience and rebellion toward His word? Vs. 19, 23.

Whose voice did Saul obey? Vs. 24

Pray to know and obey His Word.

Thoughts from Week 1

What words describe the word of the Lord in this past week's readings?

What did you learn about His Word?

What does His Word reveal about Him?

WEEK 2
1 Samuel 22 ~ 2 Chronicles 36

🕮 DAY 8

READ 2 Samuel 22:29-40

"As for God, his way is perfect; the word of the LORD is tried: he is a buckler to all them that trust in him." Vs. 31

How does our trust in the Lord relate to His word?

Compare His way to our way.

🕮 DAY 9

READ 2 Samuel 23:1-5

"The Spirit of the LORD spake by me, and his word was in my tongue." Vs. 2

Whose word; whose everlasting covenant, and whose victory? Vs. 2, 5

Pray to know and claim this everlasting covenant that is ours through Jesus Christ.

🕮 DAY 10

READ 1 Chronicles 10:1-14

"So Saul died for his transgression which he committed against the LORD, even against the word of the LORD, which he kept not, and also for asking counsel of one that had a familiar spirit, to inquire of it;" Vs. 13

What was the cause of Saul and his sons' deaths?

Pray for God to keep you faithful to His Word.

🕮 DAY 11

READ 2 Chronicles 6:1-21

"The LORD therefore hath performed his word that he hath spoken." Vs. 10

How is the Lord's word described in vs. 10, 14, 15, 17?

Pray for Him to speak to you through His Word, believing that He fulfills all that He promises.

🕮 DAY 12

READ 2 Chronicles 30:1-27

"Also in Judah the hand of God was to give them one heart to do the commandment of the king and of the princes, by the word of the LORD." Vs. 12

Where does true purification (sanctification) take place? Vs. 12, 19

Who does this? Vs. 12

Pray for God to continue to purify your heart.

🕮 DAY 13

READ 2 Chronicles 34:8-33

"Go, inquire of the LORD for me, and for them that are left in Israel and in Judah, concerning the words of the book that is found: for great is the wrath of the LORD that is poured out upon us, because our fathers have not kept the word of the LORD, to do after all that is written in this book." Vs. 21

To what is God's word referred? Vs. 14, 15, 19, 21, 27, 30

Pray for God to speak to your heart through His Word.

🕮 DAY 14

READ 2 Chronicles 36:14-23

"To fulfil the word of the LORD by the mouth of Jeremiah, until the land had enjoyed her sabbaths: for as long as she lay desolate she kept sabbath, to fulfil threescore and ten years." Vs. 21

What did the people do in response to Lord's word? vs. 16

What do verses 21 and 22 say about His word?

Pray that God's Word would be fulfilled in you.

🕮 Thoughts from Week 2

Review and record from the past week how the word of the Lord is described.

Pray according to what you have learned

WEEK 3
Psalm 12 ~ Psalm 103

Week 3

DAY 15

READ Psalm 12:1-8

"The words of the LORD are pure words: as silver tried in a furnace of earth, purified seven times." Vs. 6

How are God's words described?

What was the result of His words? Vs. 7

Pray to know the power of God's Word in your life.

DAY 16

READ Psalm 18:21-36

"As for God, his way is perfect: the word of the LORD is tried: he is a buckler to all those that trust in him." Vs. 30

Where did you read this Psalm earlier?

When did David write this Psalm?

Pray to remember the Lord's Word and His presence in difficult times.

🕮 DAY 17

READ Psalm 33:1-12

"For the word of the LORD is right;
and all his works are done in truth.
"By the word of the LORD were the heavens made;
and all the host of them by the breath of his mouth."
Vs. 4, 6

What is said of *the word of the LORD*? Vs. 4-12

What is our response? Vs. 1-3

Pray for His Word of righteousness in you.

🕮 DAY 18

READ Psalm 56:1-13

"In God I will praise his word,
 in God I have put my trust;
I will not fear what flesh can do unto me.
In God will I praise his word:
in the LORD will I praise his word." Vs. 4, 10

What is the result of God's word?

Praise God that you can trust His Word in difficult times.

🌸 DAY 19

READ Psalm 68:1-21

"The Lord gave the word: great was the company of those that published it." Vs. 11

What difference does the Lord make between the righteous and His enemies? (2, 3, 20, 21)

Pray that His Word makes a difference in your life. Praise Him for His salvation.

🌸 DAY 20

READ Psalm 78:1-22

"Give ear, O my people, to my law: incline your ears to the words of my mouth." Vs. 1

For what purpose is God's word spoken in this Psalm?

Pray to remember the truths of God's Word that have been preserved, that you may remain obedient.

🕮 DAY 21

READ Psalm 103:1-22

"Bless the LORD, ye his angels, that excel in strength, that do his commandments, hearkening unto the voice of his word." Vs. 20

What are we called to do in response to His word? Vs. 1, 2, 11, 13, 17, 18, 21

Bless the Lord and pray according to this Psalm.

🕮 Thoughts from Week 3

From this week's readings about the word of the Lord, what should we thank and praise the LORD for? What should be our responses to His Word?

What should we pray for?

WEEK 4
Psalm 105 ~ Psalm 119:80

🕮 DAY 22

READ Psalm 105:1-19

"He hath remembered his covenant for ever,
the word which he commanded to a thousand
generations." Vs. 8
"Until the time that his word came; the word of the
LORD tried him." Vs. 19

How does the Psalmist speak of God's word in this
Psalm? Vs. 5, 7, 8, 9. 10, 19

Pray to remember and tell others of God's covenant.

🕮 DAY 23

READ Psalm 107:1-22

"Because they rebelled against the words of God,
and contemned the counsel of the most High: Vs. 11
He sent his word, and healed them, and delivered *them*
 from their destructions." Vs. 20

What is the pattern revealed in these verses?

What is the response to God's goodness? 1, 2, 8, 15,
21, 22, 31

Begin to practice daily the praise that is found in
verses 8, 15, 21, 3l.

🕮 DAY 24

READ Psalm 119:1-16

"Wherewithal shall a young man cleanse his way?
by taking heed thereto according to thy word." Vs. 9
"Thy word have I hid in mine heart,
that I might not sin against thee." Vs. 11
"I will delight myself in thy statutes:
I will not forget thy word." Vs. 16

Meditate on each of these verses. Underline how each one references His word?
Where does His word work? Vs. 2, 7, 10, 11

Pray through today's reading. 1-16

🕮 DAY 25

READ Psalm 119:17-32

"Deal bountifully with thy servant, that I may live,
and keep thy word." Vs. 17
"My soul cleaveth unto the dust:
quicken thou me according to thy word." Vs. 25
"My soul melteth for heaviness:
strengthen thou me according unto thy word." Vs. 28

What is the Psalmist asking for in these verses, and how does each request relate to God's word?

Pray for strength, understanding, life, and His work in your heart according to His Word.

🌸 DAY 26

READ Psalm 119:33-48

"Stablish thy word unto thy servant,
who is devoted to thy fear." Vs. 38
"So shall I have wherewith to answer him that
reproacheth me: for I trust in thy word."
And take not the word of truth utterly out of my
mouth; for I have hoped in thy judgments." Vs. 42, 43

How is the Psalmist affected in today's reading?

Pray for these in your own heart and life.

🌸 DAY 27

READ Psalm 119:49-64

"Remember the word unto thy servant,
upon which thou hast caused me to hope." Vs. 49
"This is my comfort in my affliction:
for thy word hath quickened me." Vs. 50
"Thou art my portion, O LORD:
I have said that I would keep thy words.
I entreated thy favour with my whole heart:
be merciful unto me according to thy word."
Vs. 57, 58

How did God's Word affect David?

Pray for these things in your life.

DAY 28

READ Psalm 119:65-80

"Before I was afflicted I went astray:
but now have I kept thy word." Vs. 67

"They that fear thee will be glad when they see me;
because I have hoped in thy word."

"Let, I pray thee, thy merciful kindness be for my
comfort, according to thy word unto thy servant."
Vs. 74, 76

What are the Psalmist's comments on adversity?

How do these relate to God's word?

Thoughts from Week 4

Has this week's study caused you to see the word of the Lord differently? How has God's Word tried you this week? Have you rebelled? Have you been afflicted? How do you respond to God's Word in these circumstances?

Record and pray through the main thoughts of this past week's study.

WEEK 5
Psalm 119:81 ~ 168

DAY 29

READ Psalm 119:81-96

"My soul fainteth for thy salvation:
but I hope in thy word.
Mine eyes fail for thy word, saying,
When wilt thou comfort me?" Vs. 81, 82
For ever, O LORD, thy word is settled in heaven." Vs. 89

What is the extent of God's word in vs. 81, 92-94?

DAY 30

READ Psalm 119:97-112

"I have refrained my feet from every evil way,
that I might keep thy word." Vs. 101
"How sweet are thy words unto my taste!
yea, sweeter than honey to my mouth!" Vs. 103
"Thy word is a lamp unto my feet,
and a light unto my path." Vs. 105
"I am afflicted very much: quicken me, O LORD,
according unto thy word." Vs. 107

From David's love, meditation, and understanding of God's word, what was the result in his life? He speaks of these in almost every verse. Pray for these in your own life.

DAY 31

READ Psalm 119:113-128

"Thou art my hiding place and my shield:
I hope in thy word." Vs. 114
"Mine eyes fail for thy salvation,
and for the word of thy righteousness." Vs. 123

From David's description of His word, how do we see God? Vs. 114, 116, 117, 119, 120, 122, 124, 126

Pray to see God through His written word.

DAY 32

READ Psalm 119:129-144

"Order my steps in thy word: and let not any iniquity have dominion over me." Vs. 133
"My zeal hath consumed me,
because mine enemies have forgotten thy words.
"Thy word is very pure:
therefore, thy servant loveth it." Vs. 139, 140

Why should we love God's Word?

Pray to love and long for God's Word as David did.

🕮 DAY 33

READ Psalm 119:145-152

"I prevented the dawning of the morning, and cried:
I hoped in thy word.
Mine eyes prevent the night watches,
that I might meditate in thy word." Vs. 147, 148

How important is it to meditate on God's word?

Pray through vs. 145-152

🕮 DAY 34

READ Psalm 119:153-160

"Plead my cause, and deliver me:
 quicken me according to thy word." Vs. 154
"I beheld the transgressors, and was grieved;
because they kept not thy word." Vs. 158
"Thy word is true from the beginning:
 and every one of thy righteous judgments endureth
 for ever." Vs. 160

What is the relationship of God's word to *quickening* and *deliv*ering? Pray through these verses.

DAY 35

READ Psalm 119:161-168

"Princes have persecuted me without a cause:
but my heart standeth in awe of thy word.
"I rejoice at thy word, as one that findeth great spoil."
Vs. 161, 162

What is David's response to God's word in today's reading? Pray for these in your own life.

Thoughts from Week 5

Review and list from this week's readings God's promises and how His Word affected David's life.

Pray for these in your own life.

WEEK 6
Psalm 119:169 ~ Isaiah 28

DAY 36

READ Psalm 119:169-176

"Let my cry come near before thee, O LORD:
give me understanding according to thy word.
Let my supplication come before thee:
deliver me according to thy word. Vs. 169, 170
"My tongue shall speak of thy word:
for all thy commandments are righteousness." Vs. 172

Meditate, and pray humbly and fervently, through this reading.

DAY 37

READ Psalm 130:1-8

"I wait for the LORD, my soul doth wait,
and in his word do I hope." Vs. 5

What does the LORD's word promise in this Psalm? Vs. 7

What must we do? Vs. 1, 4, 5, 6, 7

DAY 38

READ Psalm 138:1-8

"I will worship toward thy holy temple, and praise thy name for thy lovingkindness and for thy truth: for thou hast magnified thy word above all thy name." Vs. 2

"All the kings of the earth shall praise thee, O LORD, when they hear the words of thy mouth." Vs. 4

How does David speak of the Lord in this Psalm?

What initiates His thanks and praise? Vs. 3-8

Claim the promises in vs. 7 and 8.

DAY 39

READ Psalm 147:1-20

"He sendeth forth his commandment upon earth: his word runneth very swiftly.
He sendeth out his word, and melteth them:" Vs. 15
he causeth his wind to blow, and the waters flow.
He showeth his word unto Jacob,
his statutes and his judgments unto Israel." Vs. 18, 19

Meditate on all that is spoken of the LORD in this Psalm. List the ones most relevant to you.

And praise Him!

DAY 40

READ Psalm 148:1-14

"Fire, and hail; snow, and vapour;
stormy wind fulfilling his word:" Vs. 8

Who initiates praise in this Psalm? Vs. 5, 6, 13, 14

Praise Him!

DAY 41

READ Proverbs 30:1-10

"Every word of God is pure:
he is a shield unto them that put their trust in him.
Add thou not unto his words, lest he reprove thee,
and thou be found a liar." Vs. 5, 6

Is the word of God enough? Vs. 5

Without it, or adding to it what would we have? 6, 8, 9

DAY 42

READ Isaiah 28:1-17

"But the word of the LORD was unto them precept upon precept, precept upon precept; line upon line, line upon line; here a little, and there a little; that they might go, and fall backward, and be broken, and snared, and taken." Vs. 3

"Therefore hear the word of the Lord." Vs. 14

Why did the people err? Vs. 12,14,15

What are God's promises? Vs. 5,6,9,12,16,17

Thoughts from Week 6

From this week's readings what did you learn about the Lord?

What happens when we trust in lies and falsehood?

What response does He want from us?

WEEK 7
Isaiah 30 ~ Jeremiah 8

Week 7

🕮 DAY 43

READ Isaiah 30:8-21

"Wherefore thus saith the Holy One of Israel, Because ye despise this word, and trust in oppression and perverseness, and stay thereon: Therefore this iniquity shall be to you as a breach ready to fall, swelling out in a high wall, whose breaking cometh suddenly at an instant. Vs. 12, 13

"And thine ears shall hear a word behind thee," Vs. 21

What does God's word teach us about Him in verses 18-21?

Pray to know more of His grace and mercy.

🕮 DAY 44

READ Isaiah 40:1-11

"The grass withereth, the flower fadeth:
but the word of our God shall stand for ever." Vs. 8

How are we compared to the word of our God? Vs. 6

Who speaks of the glory of the LORD? Vs. 5

Pray for the fulfillment of His promises.

🕮 DAY 45

READ Isaiah 45:9-25

"I have sworn by myself, the word is gone out of my mouth in righteousness, and shall not return, That unto me every knee shall bow, every tongue shall swear." Vs. 23

What is the purpose of God's word in these verses?
13,
17,
19,
22,
23,
24,
25
Compare Philippians 2:10-11 to vs. 23

🕮 DAY 46

READ Isaiah 55:1-13

"So shall my word be that goeth forth out of my mouth: it shall not return unto me void, but it shall accomplish that which I please, and it shall prosper in the thing whereto I sent it." Vs. 11

To what is God's word compared? 1, 2, 10

Pray for God's Word to be fruitful in you.

🕮 DAY 47

READ Isaiah 66:1-24

"For all those things hath mine hand made, and all those things have been, saith the LORD: but to this man will I look, even to him that is poor and of a contrite spirit, and trembleth at my word." Vs. 2

What difference does it make if we tremble and hear His word?
Vs. 12

Vs. 13

Vs. 14

Pray to know the peace, comfort and joy of His Word.

🕮 DAY 48

READ Jeremiah 2:1-13

"Hear ye the word of the LORD, O house of Jacob, and all the families of the house of Israel:" Vs. 4

What was word of the Lord to His people? Vs. 5-13

Pray that the Lord would keep you faithful to Him.

🕮 DAY 49

READ Jeremiah 8:1-9

"The wise men are ashamed, they are dismayed and taken: lo, they have rejected the word of the LORD; and what wisdom is in them?" Vs. 9

Of what were the people guilty? Vs. 2,5,6

Without the Lord's word, what did they lack? Vs. 9

Pray for wisdom from His Word.

🕮 Thoughts from Week 7

Pray and meditate on this past week's Bible references. Record here any special thoughts on these seven weeks' readings.

Pray for the power of the Holy Spirit to enable you to know and to keep the word of the Lord as He reveals His will to you.

WEEK 8
Jeremiah 13 ~ Jeremiah 22

Week 8

🌺 DAY 50

READ Jeremiah 13:1-14

"This evil people, which refuse to hear my words, which walk in the imagination of their heart, and walk after other gods, to serve them, and to worship them, shall even be as this girdle, which is good for nothing." Vs. 10

What does God do with that which is *good for nothing*?

Praise the Lord that He is able to keep us close to Him. Ask for His Holy Spirit for His keeping.

🌺 DAY 51

READ Jeremiah 14:1-22

"The word of the LORD that came to Jeremiah concerning the dearth." Vs. 1

"Therefore thou shalt say this word unto them; Let mine eyes run down with tears night and day, and let them not cease: for the virgin daughter of my people is broken with a great breach, with a very grievous blow." Vs. 17

Instead of God, to whom were they listening?

Pray for ears to hear His Word for you.

DAY 52

READ Jeremiah 15:1-21
"Thy words were found, and I did eat them; and thy word was unto me the joy and rejoicing of mine heart: for I am called by thy name, O LORD God of hosts."
Vs. 16

What was Jeremiah's prayer? Vs. 15-18

What was God's promise? Vs. 19-21

Pray according to God's promises.

DAY 53

READ Jeremiah 17:1-27
"Behold, they say unto me, Where is the word of the LORD? Let it come now." Vs. 15

What was His word about the Sabbath day? Vs. 21-27

Pray to keep the Lord's Day holy.

DAY 54

READ Jeremiah 18:1-17

"The word which came to Jeremiah from the LORD, saying, Arise, and go down to the potter's house, and there I will cause thee to hear my words." Vs. 1,2

In what were they trusting? Vs. 12

What was the purpose for the Lord sending Jeremiah to the potter's house?

Pray for the Lord's molding of your heart and life.

DAY 55

READ Jeremiah 20:7-13

"Then I said, I will not make mention of him, nor speak any more in his name. But his word was in mine heart as a burning fire shut up in my bones, and I was weary with forbearing, and I could not stay." Vs. 9

How powerful is the word of the LORD?
Vs. 9,
Vs. 11,
Vs. 13

Pray for the power of His Word in your heart.

🕮 DAY 56

READ Jeremiah 22:20-29
"O earth, earth, earth, hear the word of the LORD."
Vs. 29

When are we least likely to hear and obey the word of the Lord? Vs. 21

🕮 Thoughts from Week 8

What difference has the word of the Lord made in your life this past week?

Pray for more faith with the understanding that it is the power of His Word working in you. Pray that you not live by your own plans. Keep reading. Meditate on His Word. Be filled with the joy, the Holy Spirit and praise for His Word and His glory.

" The Word is so full of goodness, justice, and
sanctity, that it could be breathed from none but God.
It bears His very image.
It has no errata in it.
It is a beam of the Sun of Righteousness.
It is a crystal stream,
flowing from the Fountain of Life.
It commends to us whatever is
"just, lovely, and noble."

Thomas Watson (1620-1686)

WEEK 9
Jeremiah 23 ~ Ezekiel 36

🕮 DAY 57

READ Jeremiah 23:16-36

"For who hath stood in the counsel of the LORD, and hath perceived and heard his word? who hath marked his word, and heard it?" Vs. 18

"But if they had stood in my counsel, and had caused my people to hear my words, then they should have turned them from their evil way, and from the evil of their doings." Vs. 22

"The prophet that hath a dream, let him tell a dream; and he that hath my word, let him speak my word faithfully. Is not my word like as a fire? saith the LORD; and like a hammer that breaketh the rock in pieces?" Vs. 28, 29

Meditate, study, and find the difference between the heart, words, and result, of the prophet's, and those of the Lord. Pray for the heart of the Lord.

🕮 DAY 58

READ Jeremiah 29:8-19

"For thus saith the LORD, That after seventy years be accomplished at Babylon I will visit you, and perform my good word toward you, in causing you to return to this place." Vs. 10

What is God's promise to His people? Vs. 10-14

Pray for restoration of God's people.

DAY 59

READ Jeremiah 31:1-14

"Hear the word of the LORD, O ye nations,
and declare it in the isles afar off, and say,
He that scattered Israel will gather him,
and keep him, as a shepherd doth his flock." V 10

Meditate on the goodness of the LORD in these verses.
What relationships express His everlasting love?
Vs. 1
Vs. 9
Vs. 10
Vs. 12
Pray to know His guidance as your Shepherd.

DAY 60

READ Jeremiah 33:1-16

"Moreover the word of the LORD came unto Jeremiah the second time, while he was yet shut up in the court of the prison, saying, Thus saith the LORD the maker thereof, the LORD that formed it, to establish it; the LORD is his name; Call unto me, and I will answer thee, and show thee great and mighty things, which thou knowest not." Vs. 1-3

What words of promise did the LORD make through Jeremiah? Vs. 2, 3, 6, 7, 8, 9, 11, 12, 13, 14, 15, 16

🕮 DAY 61

READ Ezekiel 12:17-28

"Therefore say unto them, Thus saith the Lord GOD; There shall none of my words be prolonged any more, but the word which I have spoken shall be done, saith the Lord GOD." Vs. 28

How did the LORD respond in vs. 23-28 to their unbelief?

Pray according what you have read in this chapter.

🕮 DAY 62

READ Ezekiel 34:7-31

"Therefore, ye shepherds, hear the word of the LORD;" vs. 7
"And I the LORD will be their God,
and my servant David a prince among them;
I the LORD have spoken it." Vs. 24

Meditate on the promises of Lord for His sheep. Who are His sheep in this chapter?

🕮 DAY 63

READ Ezekiel 36:17-38

"Then the heathen that are left round about you shall know that I the LORD build the ruined places, and plant that that was desolate:
I the LORD have spoken it, and I will do it." Vs. 36

Why did God scatter His people? Vs. 17-18

What did they profane among the heathen? 20-23

Meditate on His promise. Vs. 23-30
What will be the result of His promise?
Vs. 31-32,
Vs. 38
Pray that you will always honor His name in your thoughts, words and actions.

🕮 Thoughts from Week 9

Record how He has been working in your heart this week.

Pray fervently for His Holy Spirit to work in you a desire for His Word and obedience to it. Record how it affects your heart and life.

WEEK 10
Ezekiel 37 ~ Zechariah 7

Week 10

🕮 DAY 64

READ Ezekiel 37:1-14

"Again he said unto me, Prophesy upon these bones, and say unto them, O ye dry bones, hear the word of the LORD." Vs. 4 "And shall put my spirit in you, and ye shall live, and I shall place you in your own land: then shall ye know that I the LORD have spoken it, and performed it, saith the LORD." Vs. 14

What is Lord's word to the *dry bones*? 5,6,8,9,10
What is this *breath* to the people of Israel? Vs. 14

How does this compare to yesterday's promise in Ezekiel 36:26-27?

🕮 DAY 65

READ Amos 8:1-14

"Behold, the days come, saith the Lord God, that I will send a famine in the land, not a famine of bread, nor a thirst for water, but of hearing the words of the LORD: And they shall wander from sea to sea, and from the north even to the east, they shall run to and fro to seek the word of the LORD and shall not find it." Vs. 11, 12

What is the worst famine that can happen to God's people?

DAY 66

READ Jonah 3:1-10

"And the word of the LORD came unto Jonah the second time, saying, Arise, go unto Nineveh, that great city, and preach unto it the preaching that I bid thee. So Jonah arose, and went unto Nineveh, according to the word of the LORD." Vs. 1-3 "For word came unto the king of Nineveh, and he arose from his throne, and he laid his robe from him, and covered him with sackcloth, and sat in ashes." Vs. 6

What was Nineveh's response to God's word?

What was the result of their repentance?

DAY 67

READ Micah 4:1-13

"And many nations shall come, and say, Come, and let us go up to the mountain of the LORD, and to the house of the God of Jacob; and he will teach us of his ways, and we will walk in his paths: for the law shall go forth of Zion, and the word of the LORD from Jerusalem." Vs. 2

Meditate on these verses and compare to Ephesians 1:15-23 and Revelation 11:15.

Where do you fit?

🕮 DAY 68

READ Haggai 2:1-9

"*According to* the word that I covenanted with you when ye came out of Egypt, so my spirit remaineth among you: fear ye not.
For thus saith the LORD of hosts; Yet once, it *is* a little while, and I will shake the heavens, and the earth, and the sea, and the dry *land;*" Vs. 5

How is the LORD going to *shake* everything? Vs. 5

With what result? Vs. 7, 9

🕮 DAY 69

READ Zechariah 4:1-14

"Then he answered and spake unto me, saying, This is the word of the LORD unto Zerubbabel, saying, Not by might, nor by power, but by my spirit, saith the LORD of hosts." Vs. 6

What will His Spirit bring? Vs. 7

Compare John 1:14, 16 and Hebrews 10:28-29

🕮 DAY 70

READ Zechariah 7:1-14

"Yea, they made their hearts as an adamant stone, lest they should hear the law, and the words which the LORD of hosts hath sent in his spirit by the former prophets:" Vs. 12

How did He send His words? Vs. 12

How did the people respond?

Compare vs. 13 with Jonah 3:10. What was the difference?

🕮 Thoughts from Week 10

What promises did you claim from the readings of the past week? How do you see these everlasting promises fulfilled in Jesus Christ?

Pray to know the LORD's goodness in your own life as He has promised His people through His written word.

WEEK 11
Zechariah 11 ~ Mark 7

DAY 71

READ Zechariah 11:1-17

"And it was broken in that day and so the poor of the flock that waited upon me knew that it was the word of the LORD." Vs. 11

How is the shepherd described in vs. 17?

Compare with John 10:1-18

DAY 72

READ Zechariah 12:1-13:1

"The burden of the word of the LORD for Israel, saith the LORD,
which stretcheth forth the heavens,
and layeth the foundation of the earth,
and formeth the spirit of man within him." Vs. 1

What is the meaning of the word "burden" in vs. 1 and 3?

What is said of the spirit in vs. 10?

Compare vs. 10 to John 19:37 and Psalm 22:16.

> ### 📖 Thoughts from the Old Testament
>
> What stands out in these last few readings? What are the prophecies most concerning?
>
> Take some extra time to review before beginning the New Testament references.

NEW TESTAMENT

📖 DAY 73

READ Matthew 3:13-4:11

"But he answered and said,
"It is written, Man shall not live by bread alone,
but by every word that proceedeth out of the mouth of God." Vs. 4

What two things did Jesus have with which to defend Himself?

How are we to live? Vs. 4

Week 11

🕮 DAY 74

READ Matthew 8:1-17

"The centurion answered and said, Lord, I am not worthy that thou shouldest come under my roof: but speak the word only, and my servant shall be healed." Vs. 8

When was the servant healed? Vs. 8, 13

🕮 DAY 75

READ Mark 2:1-12

"And straightway many were gathered together, insomuch that there was no room to receive them, no, not so much as about the door: and he preached the word unto them." Vs. 2

As Jesus preached the word what was the result? Vs. 5, 10-12

DAY 76

READ Mark 4:26-34
"And with many such parables spake he the word unto them, as they were able to hear it." Vs. 33

What is the relationship of the word to the kingdom of God? Vs. 26,
27,
31,
32

DAY 77

READ Mark 7:1-13
"Making the word of God of none effect through your tradition, which ye have delivered: and many such like things do ye." Vs. 13

How did the Pharisees make the word of God ineffective?

Vs. 7,
9,
13

> Record your first impressions from Jesus' ministry of the Word.

WEEK 12
Mark 16 ~ Luke 4

DAY 78

Mark 16:1-20

"And they went forth, and preached every where, the Lord working with them, and confirming the word with signs following. Amen." Vs. 20

What followed Jesus' resurrection? Vs. 15-20

How did the Lord work with them? Acts **8**4:8

DAY 79

READ Luke 1:1-25

"Even as they delivered them unto us, which from the beginning were eyewitnesses, and ministers of the word;" Vs. 2

How would John turn the children of Israel to the Lord? Vs. 15,17 Compare Malachi 4:5-6

Why was Zacharias made dumb? Vs. 1:20

What does God give with His word to make it effective?

What do these two work in the heart of the hearer?

DAY 80

READ Luke 1:26-38

"And Mary said, Behold the handmaid of the Lord; be it unto me according to thy word. And the angel departed from her." Vs. 38

How did God speak to Mary? Vs. 1,38

What was her response? 29, 34, 38

How did she and we receive Christ? 35, 38

DAY 81

READ Luke 2:21-35

"Lord, now lettest thou thy servant depart in peace, according to thy word:" Vs. 9

Why did Joseph and Mary bring Jesus to the temple? 21-24

Why was Simeon there? 25-32

Who did he bless first? 28, 34

🕮 DAY 82

READ Luke 3:1-17

"Annas and Caiaphas being the high priests, the word of God came unto John the son of Zacharias in the wilderness." Vs. 2

To whom was the word of God given---the high priest or John? What was the word he came to preach? 3

What would be proof of repentance? 11, 13, 14

Was repentance and their works and obedience to the law their salvation? Vs. 6
Compare to Luke 2:26, 30-32
Compare 9 with Luke 2: 34-35
How does salvation come? Vs. 16

Compare to John 3:5 and Romans 2:4

🕮 DAY 83

READ Luke 4:14-32

"And they were astonished at his doctrine: for his word was with power." Vs. 32

What was the difference in Jesus's teaching in Nazareth in 16-30 and in Capernaum?31-32

What was the difference in the responses?

DAY 84

READ Luke 4:33-44

"And they were all amazed, and spake among themselves, saying, What a word is this! for with authority and power he commandeth the unclean spirits, and they come out." Vs. 6

How is the word of God used by Christ? 34, 35, 36, 39, 41, 43, 44. Compare 1 John 3:8

How did the demons identify Him? 34, 41

Thoughts for Week 12

Review the different ways through which the word of God has come.

Which of these do we have today?

Who fulfilled the word and the prophecies?

How are we enabled to hear and receive Christ as our Savior?

WEEK 13
Luke 8 ~ John 2

DAY 85

READ Luke 8:1-18

"Now the parable is this: The seed is the word of God.
"But that on the good ground are they,
which in an honest and good heart,
having heard the word, keep *it*,
and bring forth fruit with patience." Vs. 11, 15

What was the word of God that Jesus preached and showed? Vs. 1 Compare Matthew 4:23

Who *brought forth fruit*? Vs. 1, 2, 8, 10, 18 Compare Isaiah 55:10-13.

DAY 86

READ Luke 10:38-42

"And she had a sister called Mary, which also sat at Jesus' feet, and heard his word." Vs. 39

What was Martha's greatest need---and ours? Compare Jesus' words in Matthew 6:32-34.

DAY 87

READ Luke 11:14-28

"But he said, Yea rather, blessed are they that hear the word of God, and keep it." Vs. 28

What happened in this passage of God's word?

How does verse 28 relate to this passage?

Meditate and pray for wisdom from Jesus' words.

DAY 88

READ Luke 22:31-62

"And the Lord turned, and looked upon Peter. And Peter remembered the word of the Lord, how he had said unto him, Before the cock crow, thou shalt deny me thrice." Vs. 61

What happened between verses 31 and 62?

What is Jesus doing as an example for His disciples and us? 40-46

What was He facing, and soon to conquer, for us? Vs. 53

What is accomplished by His prayer? 32, 37, 42

🕮 DAY 89

READ Luke 24:13-49

"And he said unto them, What things? And they said unto him, Concerning Jesus of Nazareth, which was a prophet mighty in deed and word before God and all the people:" Vs. 19

Even as witnesses were they able to see and believe? 16, 36-38, 41, 45, 48
What things did Jesus say had been fulfilled, that were written of and spoken by Him? 44-49

What further promise did He give them? 49

🕮 DAY 90

READ John 1:1-18

"In the beginning was the Word, and the Word was with God, and the Word was God." Vs. 1
"And the Word was made flesh, and dwelt among us, (and we beheld his glory, the glory as of the only begotten of the Father,) full of grace and truth." Vs. 14

To what does the Word refer? 3,4,7,10

What else describes this person? 4,7

Of these three which is first? Vs. 1 (See Genesis 1:3)

🕮 DAY 91

READ John 2:13-22

"When therefore he was risen from the dead, his disciples remembered that he had said this unto them; and they believed the scripture, and the word which Jesus had said." Vs. 22

What had the temple become? Vs. 16

What was the difference in the Father's earthly temple and Christ's body? 19, 21 (See Revelation 21:10, 22)

What did the disciples remember? 17, 22

🕮 Thoughts for Week 13

Record your impressions from this week's readings.

WEEK 14
John 4 ~ John 8

🕮 DAY 92

READ John 4:3-42

"And many more believed because of his own word; And said unto the woman, Now we believe, not because of thy saying: for we have heard him ourselves, and know that this is indeed the Christ, the Saviour of the world." Vs. 41

Meditate on these verses, especially Jesus' words. What do you believe?

🕮 DAY 93

READ John 4:43-53

"Jesus saith unto him, Go thy way; thy son liveth. And the man believed the word that Jesus had spoken unto him, and he went his way." Vs. 50

What effect did Jesus' word have on the father? 50

On His son?
On His household?
What difference do words make?

What is the significance of "the Word" compared to words?

Look up "word" from John 1:1 in a concordance to find the meaning. Pray to hear and keep His word by the power of His Holy Spirit.

🕮 DAY 94

READ John 5:17-29

"Verily, verily, I say unto you, He that heareth my word, and believeth on him that sent me, hath everlasting life, and shall not come into condemnation but is passed from death unto life." Vs. 24

How close are the Father and the Son?

What is the purpose of hearing and believing? 24

🕮 DAY 95

READ John 5:30-47

"For had ye believed Moses, ye would have believed me: for he wrote of me.
But if ye believe not his writings, how shall ye believe my words?" Vs. 46, 47

To what did the scriptures bear witness? Vs. 39

What was the purpose of His words? 34,40

Week 14

🕮 DAY 96

READ John 6:44-69

"It is the spirit that quickeneth; the flesh profiteth nothing; the words that I speak unto you, they are spirit, and they are life." Then Simon Peter answered him, Lord, to whom shall we go? Thou hast the words of eternal life." Vs. 63, 68

What truth of the Father's covenant do we find in verses 44, 45 and 65?

Meditate and explain Jesus' meaning of verses 53-58.

🕮 DAY 97

READ John 8:13-36

"Then said Jesus to those Jews which believed on him, If ye continue in my word, *then* are ye my disciples indeed; And ye shall know the truth, and the truth shall make you free." Vs. 31,32

What is the proof of a true disciple? Vs. 31

What do we find in His word? 32

What shall we be freed from by the truth? 24, 34

DAY 98

READ John 8:37-51

"He that is of God heareth God's words: ye therefore hear them not, because ye are not of God." Vs. 47

What does unbelief seek to do with the truth?
40,
44-46

See Genesis 3:1-6, 13

Thoughts for Week 14

What was Jesus' claim that the religious leaders could not accept? How are lies and sin related?

WEEK 15
John 10 ~ John 17

🕮 DAY 99

READ John 10:22-42

"If he called them gods, unto whom the word of God came, and the scripture cannot be broken;" Vs. 35

What was the purpose of their asking in verses 24, 31, 39?
Meditate on the truth of Jesus' words and works. What promises can we claim in these verses?

🕮 DAY 100

READ John 12:37-51

"And if any man hear my words, and believe not, I judge him not: for I came not to judge the world, but to save the world. He that rejecteth me, and receiveth not my words, hath one that judgeth him: the word that I have spoken, the same shall judge him in the last day." Vs. 47, 48

How will we be judged in the last day? 47,48 How are Jesus' words relative to Himself? 48

To what is His word referred in 49, 50?

What does His word command? 50
Compare John 1:1-14 (Day 90) What three words do you find in both chapters?

DAY 101

READ John 15:1-16
"Now ye are clean through the word which I have spoken unto you." Vs. 3

Meditate on these verses, praying for an understanding of the work of His word in you. Vs. 3, 6, 9, 10, 12, 14 Believe the words of vs. 16.

DAY 102

READ John 15:16-27
"Remember the word that I said unto you, The servant is not greater than his lord. If they have persecuted me, they will also persecute you; if they have kept my saying, they will keep yours also." Vs. 20

What does Jesus say about Himself in each of these verses?

Who are the persons mentioned in verse 26?

See John 14:16,17,26 and 16:7-13

🕮 DAY 103

READ John 17:1-10

"I have manifested thy name unto the men which thou gavest me out of the world: thine they were, and thou gavest them me; and they have kept thy word." For I have given unto them the words which thou gavest me; and they have received *them*, and have known surely that I came out from thee, and they have believed that thou didst send me." Vs. 6, 8

What is Jesus' power? Vs. 2
What is life eternal? Vs. 3
Who receives eternal life? Vs.2, 6
How? Vs. 6, 8, 9 (See Psalm 138:2, 4)

🕮 DAY 104

READ John 17:11-20

"I have given them thy word; and the world hath hated them, because they are not of the world, even as I am not of the world." Vs. 14
"Sanctify them through thy truth: thy word is truth." Vs. 17

How had Jesus *kept* His disciples? What *name*? Vs. 11
What other word refers to being *kept*? Vs. 17,19
How are we set apart (*sanctified*) with Christ? See John 1:1,14, 17; 14:6; 16:13,14 24 See Hebrews 2:11-14; Ephesians 5:25-26; 1 Thessalonians 5:23-24
2 Thessalonians 2:13; 1 Peter 1:2

DAY 105

READ John 17:20-26
"Neither pray I for these alone, but for them also which shall believe on me through their word;" Vs. 20

What is Jesus' prayer for us? Vs. 20, 21

What is the union for which Jesus prays---with Him, the Father and one another? Vs. 13, 23, 24, 26

See Romans 5:5 Ephesians 3:17 and Colossians 1:27

Thoughts for Week 15

How are unbelief and death related?

How are Jesus' words and life related?

Pray to be a true disciple, continuing in His word, knowing the truth, abiding in Him and being set free from all bondage.

WEEK 16
Acts 2 ~ Acts 8

🕮 DAY 106

READ Acts 2:21-42

"And with many other words did he testify and exhort, saying, Save yourselves from this untoward generation. Then they that gladly received his word were baptized: and the same day there were added *unto them* about three thousand souls." Vs. 40, 41

What is the promise in verse 21?

Meditate on the words the men of Israel were told to hear---22-36. What was their response? Vs. 37

What were they told to do? 38-40

What were the results? 41-42

🕮 DAY 107

READ Acts 4:1-22

"Howbeit many of them which heard the word believed; and the number of the men was about five thousand." Vs. 4

How was Peter able to speak boldly? Vs. 8, 13

What name does he preach? 10-12

How is healing related to salvation? Vs. 9, 12

DAY 108

READ Acts 4:13-30

"And now, Lord, behold their threatenings: and grant unto thy servants, that with all boldness they may speak thy word," Vs. 29

How is the name of Jesus relative to God's Word and to the work of His disciples? Vs. 17, 18, 19, 20, 21, 24, 25, 27, 29, 30

DAY 109

READ Acts 4:31-37

"And when they had prayed, the place was shaken where they were assembled together; and they were all filled with the Holy Ghost, and they spake the word of God with boldness." Vs. 31

How powerful was the Holy Ghost in the word and prayer?

Week 16

🕮 DAY 110

READ Acts 6:1-8

"And the word of God increased; and the number of the disciples multiplied in Jerusalem greatly; and a great company of the priests were obedient to the faith." Vs. 7

What was the effect of the Holy Ghost and the word in today's reading?

🕮 DAY 111

READ Acts 8:1-17

"Therefore they that were scattered abroad went everywhere preaching the word." Vs. 4

How are verses 4, 12, 14, synonymous?

What accompanies the word? Vs. 16, 17

Why was the word preached everywhere? Vs. 1, 4

DAY 112

READ Acts 8:25-39

"And they, when they had testified and preached the word of the Lord, returned to Jerusalem, and preached the gospel in many villages of the Samaritans." Vs. 25

What is relative to the word in verses 25, 30, 32, 35?

What was the result of Philip's preaching? Vs. 36-37

What is required before baptism? Vs. 37

What was Philip's power and guidance? Vs. 26, 29, 39

Thoughts for Week 16

How do you see the fulfillment of Jesus' words in the work of Peter and the disciples?

Where do you see the message of the Trinity (Father, Son, and Holy Ghost) in this week's reading---names, work, etc.?

How are you seeing the power of His word and Spirit in you?

WEEK 17
Acts 10 ~ Acts 17

🕮 DAY 113

READ Acts 10:1-48

"The word which *God* sent unto the children of Israel, preaching peace by Jesus Christ: (he is Lord of all:)" Vs. 36
"While Peter yet spake these words, the Holy Ghost fell on all them which heard the word." Vs. 44

Why was Peter sent to Cornelius' house? Vs. 33

What was the word of truth that Peter spoke? Vs. 34-43

What was the effect? Vs. 44-48

🕮 DAY 114

READ Acts 11:1-18

"And the apostles and brethren that were in Judaea heard that the Gentiles had also received the word of God." Vs. 1
"Then remembered I the word of the Lord, how that he said, John indeed baptized with water; but ye shall be baptized with the Holy Ghost." Vs. 16

How is the word fulfilled in verses 15-16?

To what is the word referred? Vs. 14, 17, 18

🕮 DAY 115

READ Acts 12:1-25
"But the word of God grew and multiplied." Vs. 24

What were the circumstances in which *the word of God grew and multiplied?*

🕮 DAY 116

READ Acts 13:38-52
"And the next sabbath day came almost the whole city together to hear the word of God." Vs. 44
"And the word of the Lord was published throughout all the region." Vs. 49

What is the difference in the response of the Gentiles and the Jews to the *preaching* of the word of God? Vs.42-45, 48, 50

How did the Lord plan for the word to extend to other nations? Vs. 46, 47, 49

How were Paul and Barnabas affected by the persecution? 50-52

DAY 117

READ Acts 14:1-28

"Long time therefore abode they speaking boldly in the Lord, which gave testimony unto the word of his grace, and granted signs and wonders to be done by their hands." Vs. 3

To what is the word referred in verses 3, 7, 2?

Through their experiences, what truth did Paul teach? Vs. 22

What else did he and Barnabas do? Vs. 22, 23

DAY 118

READ Acts 16:14-34

"And they spake unto him the word of the Lord, and to all that were in his house." Vs. 32

What is the effect of the word? Vs. 14-15, 18, 25-34

What accompanies the preaching of God's word? Vs. 15, 16, 25, 33

Who was saved and baptized? Vs. 15, 31, 32, 33, 34

DAY 119

READ Acts 17:1-14

"These were more noble than those in Thessalonica, in that they received the word with all readiness of mind, and searched the scriptures daily, whether those things were so." Vs. 11

What did Paul use to preach Christ? Vs. 2, 3

How were the Bereans confirmed in the truth? Vs. 11 See John 5:39; 8:31-32

Thoughts for Week 17

Review and meditate on the truths of this week's reading. Record your impressions. Pray for the power of the word and the Holy Spirit in your heart and life.

WEEK 18
Acts 18 ~ Romans 8

🕮 DAY 120

READ Acts 18:1-11

"And he continued *there* a year and six months, teaching the word of God among them." Vs. 11

What was the testimony that the Jews in Corinth opposed? Vs. 5-6

What about others? Vs. 8

What enabled Paul to preach the word? Vs. 9-10

🕮 DAY 121

READ Acts 18:24-19:10

"And this continued by the space of two years; so that all they which dwelt in Asia heard the word of the Lord Jesus, both Jews and Greeks." Vs. 10

To what does the word refer in verses 25, 26, 9?

Around whom does the entire word center? 28, 4, 5, 10

How do we believe? Vs. 27 See Ephesians 2:4, 5, 8, 9.

🕮 DAY 122

READ Acts 19:13-20

"So mightily grew the word of God and prevailed." Vs. 20

What was the power sought and magnified?

What was the result? Vs. 18-19

What grew and prevailed? Vs. 20

🕮 DAY 123

READ Acts 20: 17-35

"And now, brethren, I commend you to God, and to the word of his grace, which is able to build you up, and to give you an inheritance among all them which are sanctified." Vs. 32

Meditate on Paul's ministry of the gospel.
How did Paul describe the work of the gospel? Vs. 21, 24, 25, 27, 32

What did it cost him? 19, 20, 22-25

What was his warning? 28-35 (See 1 Peter 5: 10-12)

Week 18

🕮 DAY 124

READ Romans 9:1-26

"Not as though the word of God hath taken none effect. For they *are* not all Israel, which are of Israel:" Vs. 6

By what power does the word take effect? Vs. 11, 16, 17, 23, 24

For what purpose? Vs. 17, 24-25

🕮 DAY 125

READ Romans 10:1-13

"But what saith it? The word is nigh thee, *even* in thy mouth, and in thy heart: that is, the word of faith, which we preach;" Vs. 8

Look for the words "saved" and "salvation." Vs. 1, 9, 10, 13
How is the word described? Vs. 8

Follow the path of "the word of faith which we preach." Vs. 4, 6,
Where does this faith begin? 1, 6, 8, 9,10

Where does it work out? Vs. 8, 9, 10, 12, 13

DAY 126

READ Romans 10:14-21

"So then faith *cometh* by hearing, and hearing by the word of God." Vs. 17

How is the word described? Vs. 15, 16, 17

How does faith come?

What is needful for salvation? Vs. 14-15

How far have the words gone?

Thoughts for Week 18

Review and record your thoughts about Paul and the disciples concerning the power and effect of the word of the Lord.

How does what you have learned affect your relationship to the word and to Jesus Christ, Himself.

Pray according to what you have learned.

WEEK 19
Romans 15 ~ Galatians 5

DAY 127

READ Romans 15:1-21

"For I will not dare to speak of any of those things which Christ hath not wrought by me, to make the Gentiles obedient, by word and deed," Vs. 18

What was the result of Paul's preaching the word? Vs. 4, 5-8, 9-12, 13-14, 17-21

Compare vs. 18 to Romans 1:5 and 16:26
What is the result of faith in relation to God?

DAY 128

READ 1 Corinthians 12:1-14

"For to one is given by the Spirit the word of wisdom; to another the word of knowledge by the same Spirit;" Vs. 8

What is the work of the Holy Spirit in these verses?

What is the source of the Spirit? Vs. 5, 6,

To whom are spiritual gifts given? Vs. 11

For what purpose? Vs. 7, 12-13

DAY 129

READ 2 Corinthians 2:9-17

"For we are not as many, which corrupt the word of God: but as of sincerity, but as of God, in the sight of God speak we in Christ." Vs. 17

How is the word of God related to Christ? Vs. 10, 12, 14, 15, 17

DAY 130

READ 2 Corinthians 5:1-21

"To wit, that God was in Christ, reconciling the world unto himself, not imputing their trespasses unto them; and hath committed unto us the word of reconciliation." Vs. 19

What is *the terror of the Lord*? Vs. 10, 11, 12

What two things speak of Christ? Vs. 10, 14

What affect does *the love of Christ* have? Vs. 14, 15

How does knowing Christ affect us? Vs. 16, 17

To what is the word referred? Vs. 18-20

What exchange is made for us in Christ? Vs. 21

📖 DAY 131

READ 2 Corinthians 6:1-18

"By the word of truth, by the power of God, by the armour of righteousness on the right hand and on the left," Vs. 7

How does the righteousness in 2 Corinthians 5:21 come to us? 6:1
To what is the word referred? Vs. 1, 2

Is salvation for only one day? Vs. 2
How did they receive righteousness and *the grace of God in vain*? Vs. 14

How did Paul command them to *be enlarged*? Vs. 13, 17

What claim does the grace of God have on believers? Vs. 18

📖 DAY 132

READ 2 Corinthians 13:1-14

"This *is* the third *time* I am coming to you. In the mouth of two or three witnesses shall every word be established." Vs. 1

What is proof of the word? Vs. 1, 3, 4, 5, 7, 8, 10, 11, 14

DAY 133

READ Galatians 5:1-26

"For all the law is fulfilled in one word, *even* in this; Thou shalt love thy neighbour as thyself." Vs. 14

What does the word work in us? Vs. 1, 4, 5, 6, 13, 16

Through whom does the word work? Vs. 25

How does the Spirit work liberty, faith, and love? Vs. 17, 18, 22-26

Thoughts for the Week 19

How do you see the grace of God working by the Holy Spirit to apply the word of God to our hearts and lives?
What is "grace?"

Do we deserve salvation?
Do we have any control over God's word or His grace?
Who is able to hear God's word and believe?

Pray for more of His saving grace, more faith, and obedience to His word.

WEEK 20
Galatians 6 ~ Colossians 1

🕮 DAY 134

READ Galatians 6:1-18

"Let him that is taught in the word communicate unto him that teacheth in all good things." Vs. 6

Who are the *spiritual*? Vs. 1 (See 5:18, 22, 23, 25; 6:8, 9, 10, 15)

How did Paul see himself? Vs. 14, 15

🕮 DAY 135

READ Ephesians 1:1-23

"In whom ye also *trusted*, after that ye heard the word of truth, the gospel of your salvation: in whom also after that ye believed, ye were sealed with that holy Spirit of promise," Vs. 13

When did God choose to bless us *in Christ*? Vs. 3-5

For what purpose? Vs. 6, 12, 13, 14
To what is His word and work referred? Vs. 8, 9, 11, 13, 17, 18, 19
How was *the greatness of His power* demonstrated? Vs. 20-21
To whom has He given this power vs. 22

Where do you fit in? vs. 23, 10 (See Colossians 1:20 and Ephesians 2:1-10)

DAY 136

READ Ephesians 5:21-33

"That he might sanctify and cleanse it with the washing of water by the word," Vs. 26

What does Christ do through the word? Vs. 26, 27

What did He do first? Vs. 25

How close are we to Christ? Vs. 30

How does the word work through a husband?

DAY 137

READ Ephesians 6:1-20

"And take the helmet of salvation, and the sword of the Spirit, which is the word of God:" Vs. 17

What do we wrestle against? Vs. 11, 12

How do we wrestle? Vs. 10, 11

Name the parts of armour. Vs. 14-17

Where have we learned about this armour?

Why was Paul in bonds? Vs. 19-20

With the weapons of our warfare in hand, so to speak, what else are we to do? Vs. 18

DAY 138

READ Philippians 1:10-30

"And many of the brethren in the Lord, waxing confident by my bonds, are much more bold to speak the word without fear." Vs. 14

What result did Paul want to see from the Philippians? Vs. 10, 19, 26-30

What was the result of his preaching the gospel? Vs. 13 14, 20 (See vs. 7)

DAY 139

READ Philippians 2:1-21

"Holding forth the word of life; that I may rejoice in the day of Christ, that I have not run in vain, neither laboured in vain." Vs. 16

Read these verses with an understanding of Paul's association to Christ's humility and suffering. Then go back and read through Chapter 1, looking for all references to Christ.
See Paul's position.

🕮 DAY 140

READ Colossians 1:1-29

"For the hope which is laid up for you in heaven, whereof ye heard before in the word of the truth of the gospel;" Vs. 5

"Whereof I am made a minister, according to the dispensation of God which is given to me for you, to fulfil the word of God;" vs. 25

What are the references to *the word*? Vs. 5, 6, 10, 23, 25-27

What are the references to *Christ* and *the Son*?

Where are you in this chapter?

🕮 Thoughts for Week 20

You have been challenged this week to see whether you live *by the flesh* or *by the Spirit*.

Review and pray and seek the Father's heart, *the counsel of His will* to work in your heart to assure you of His Holy Spirit, and to deliver you from any sin that He reveals.

WEEK 21
Colossians 3 ~ 1 Timothy 3

🕮 DAY 141

READ Colossians 3:1-17

"Let the word of Christ dwell in you richly in all wisdom; teaching and admonishing one another in psalms and hymns and spiritual songs, singing with grace in your hearts to the Lord. And whatsoever ye do in word or deed, *do* all in the name of the Lord Jesus, giving thanks to God and the Father by him." Vs. 16, 17

What are the commands for our living? vs. 1-3, 5, 8, 12-17

Where is the *peace of God* and *the word of Christ*?

How? Vs. 10 (See Ephesians 4:21-24 and Romans 12:1-2)

🕮 DAY 142

READ 1 Thessalonians 1:1-10

"For our gospel came not unto you in word only, but also in power, and in the Holy Ghost, and in much assurance;as ye know what manner of men we were among you for your sake. And ye became followers of us, and of the Lord, having received the word in much affliction, with joy of the Holy Ghost:" Vs. 5, 6

"For from you sounded out the word of the Lord not only in Macedonia and Achaia, but also in every place your faith to God-ward is spread abroad; so that we need not to speak any thing." Vs. 8

How did the *gospel* come? Vs. 5

With what results? Vs. 6, 3, 7, 8, 9-10

DAY 143

READ 1 Thessalonians 2:1-20

"For this cause also thank we God without ceasing, because, when ye received the word of God which ye heard of us, ye received *it* not *as* the word of men, but as it is in truth, the word of God, which effectually worketh also in you that believe." Vs. 13

How does this chapter speak of *the word*? Vs. 2, 4, 8, 9, 13

What is the purpose of Paul's speaking? Vs. 12, 16

How did he minister to them? Vs. 2, 4, 7, 8, 10, 11

At what risk? Vs. 2, 14, 15

What reward? Vs. 12, 19, 20

🕮 DAY 144

READ 1 Thessalonians 3:13-4:18
"For this we say unto you by the word of the Lord, that we which are alive *and* remain unto the coming of the Lord shall not prevent them which are asleep." Vs. 15

What is the end result of the word (*the gospel*) Paul preached? Vs. 3:13, 4:7

What did they receive from Paul? Vs. 1, 2-4, 11-12

What was the hope given by *the word of the Lord*? Vs. 13-18
To what are we called? Vs. 7 (See 1 Peter 5:10)

🕮 DAY 145

READ 2 Thessalonians 2:1-17
"Therefore, brethren, stand fast, and hold the traditions which ye have been taught, whether by word, or our epistle." Vs. 15

Who shall be *destroyed* and *damned*? Vs. 8, 10-12
How and when did God choose us *to salvation*? Vs. 13
How are we *called*? Vs. 14-15
What is the work of *the Lord Jesus, and God, the Father*? Vs. 16-17 See Philippians 2:13 Colossians 1:29 Ephesians 1:19; 3:20 Philippians 1:6; Hebrews 13:20-21

DAY 146

READ 2 Thessalonians 3:1-18
"Finally, brethren, pray for us, that the word of the Lord may have *free* course, and be glorified, even as *it is* with you:" Vs. 1

What is the work of the Lord? Vs. 3, 4, 5, 6, 12, 16, 18

What prayer does Paul ask? 1, 2

DAY 147

READ 1 Timothy 3:15-4:16
"For it is sanctified by the word of God and prayer.
If thou put the brethren in remembrance of these things, thou shalt be a good minister of Jesus Christ, nourished up in the words of faith and of good doctrine, whereunto thou hast attained." 4:5, 6

What is *the church*? 3:15

In whom was *godliness* revealed? 3:16

What was Paul's instruction to Timothy? Vs. 7-8, 15-16 (See 2 Peter 1:3-4)

Review, pray and ask for the Holy Spirit to give you the main thoughts for this past week.

WEEK 22
2 Timothy 2 ~ Hebrews 4

🕮 DAY 148

READ 2 Timothy 2:1-21

"Wherein I suffer trouble, as an evil doer, *even* unto bonds; but the word of God is not bound." Vs. 9

Why did Paul instruct Timothy to be *strong* and to *endure*? Vs. 1-3, 8-10

What did he instruct him in vs. 14-16

What is the *seal of the foundation of God*? Vs. 19

What is the *nature of a vessel of honor*? Vs. 19, 21 (See 1 John 3:1-3)

🕮 DAY 149

READ 2 Timothy 4:1-8

"Preach the word; be instant in season, out of season; reprove, rebuke, exhort with all longsuffering and doctrine." Vs. 2

How is the Lord Jesus described? Vs. 1, 8

What is the charge given to Timothy? Vs. 2-4

How is the word described? Vs. 2-3, 4

What relationship does Jesus the righteous judge have to this charge? (See John 12:42-48 and John 5:24)

DAY 150

READ Titus 1:1-16

"But hath in due times manifested his word through preaching, which is committed unto me according to the commandment of God our Saviour;" Vs. 3
"Holding fast the faithful word as he hath been taught, that he may be able by sound doctrine both to exhort and to convince the gainsayers." Vs. 9

Follow through verses 1-3 and find the references to, or the effect of, the word.

For what purpose was Titus left in Crete? Vs. 5

What was the *elders'* duty to the word? Vs. 9

Who were the *gainsayers*? Vs. 10-13, 14-16

DAY 151

READ Titus 2:1-15

"*To be* discreet, chaste, keepers at home, good, obedient to their own husbands, that the word of God be not blasphemed." Vs. 5

What instruction does Paul give concerning *sound doctrine*? Vs. 1, 7-8, 9-10, 15

What was the sound doctrine to the *aged men*? Vs. 1-2

To *aged women*? Vs. 3-5

For what purpose? Vs. 5-6

To *young men*? Vs. 6

Meditate on verses 11-14, following the path of *God's grace* to its power and purpose for all. (See Ephesians 5:25-27)

DAY 152

READ Hebrews 1:1-14

"Who being the brightness of *his* glory, and the express image of his person, and upholding all things by the word of his power, when he had by himself purged our sins, sat down on the right hand of the Majesty on high;" Vs. 3

Through whom did God first speak? Vs. 1

Through whom does He now speak? Vs. 2

What is the relationship of the Father to the Son? Vs. 2-3, 5

How is the Son greater than the angels? Vs. 2-4, 5-6, 8-9, 13

How is He greater than the creation? Vs. 3, 10-12

By what power does He uphold all things? Vs. 3

What is the role of angels? Vs. 6, 7, 14 (See Psalm 34:7; 103:20)

📖 DAY 153

READ Hebrews 2:1-18

"For if the word spoken by angels was stedfast, and every transgression and disobedience received a just recompense of reward; How shall we escape, if we neglect so great salvation; which at the first began to be spoken by the Lord, and was confirmed unto us by them that heard *him*," Vs. 2-3

Why should we *take earnest heed to the things we have heard* and read? Vs. 1-3 (See 1:11-12)

How much greater is man than the angels? Vs. 3-8

What is this *great salvation*? 3, 9-10

What is Jesus, *who made the world and upholds all things by His power*, to man? Vs. 11-13

Why was Jesus a man and not an angel? Vs. 14-17

What does He do for us now? Vs. 18 (See Hebrews 4: 14-16)

🕮 DAY 154

READ [Hebrews 4:1-16](#)

"For unto us was the gospel preached, as well as unto them:but the word preached did not profit them, not being mixed with faith in them that heard *it*." Vs. 2
"For the word of God *is* quick, and powerful, and sharper than any twoedged sword, piercing even to the dividing asunder of soul and spirit, and of the joints and marrow, and *is* a discerner of the thoughts and intents of the heart." Vs. 12

When did God rest? Vs. 4

How do we rest from our work? Vs. 1-3, 10

Where is our faith tested and made known? Vs. 7, 12

By what power? Vs. 12

🕮 Thoughts for Week 22

Review the references from this week's readings that pertain to God's *calling, sanctification, holiness,* and *godliness*.

How do you understand and relate to these?

Are these your work, or the Lord's?

Pray for this effectual working of His Spirit in you as His *vessel of honor*.

WEEK 23
Hebrews 5 ~ Hebrews 13

🕮 DAY 155

READ Hebrews 5:1-14

"For every one that useth milk *is* unskilful in the word of righteousness: for he is a babe. But strong meat belongeth to them that are of full age, *even* those who by reason of use have their senses exercised to discern both good and evil." Vs. 13, 14

How is Christ's priesthood like Aaron's? Vs. 4-5

How is it different? Vs. 1-3, 6-10

How are we like Jesus, our High Priest? Vs. 8-9

To what is *the word* referred in verses 12, 13?

How are those who are *teachers*, skillful *in the word of righteousness* described? Vs. 14

🕮 DAY 156

READ Hebrews 6:1-20

"And have tasted the good word of God, and the powers of the world to come," Vs. 5

When the word of God is effective to *salvation* what will be the result? Vs. 9-12

When do we *obtain the promise*? Vs. 11, 12, 15

How are we *heirs of the promise*? Vs. 16-18

To what is God's word referenced in verse 17?

How is our *hope* in *the immutability of his counsel* described? Vs. 11, 18, 19

Through whom was this hope obtained? Vs. 20

DAY 157

READ Hebrews 7:1-28

"For the law maketh men high priests which have infirmity; but the word of the oath, which was since the law, *maketh* the Son, who is consecrated for evermore." Vs. 28

What is the difference between the old priesthood and the priesthood of Christ? Vs. 14-16, 23-24, 27

How does this affect the law? Vs. 12, 18-22

How does it affect our relationship with God? Vs. 19, 25-27

Week 23

🕮 DAY 158

READ Hebrews 10:35-11:39

"Through faith we understand that the worlds were framed by the word of God, so that things which are seen were not made of things which do appear." Vs. 3

Meditate on 10:35-39. Bridge chapter 10 to chapter 11 with verses 1-3.

As you think of verses 3 --- the beginning of God's word in creation --- follow the faith of each character.

What do you see in their *faith*, the *promise* and the *reward*? 10:36, 11:6, 7, 8, 9, 11, 13, 17, 24-27, 32-33, 35, 39

What was the *thing hoped for, not yet seen*? Vs. 10, 14-16, 35

🕮 DAY 159

READ Hebrews 11:40-12:21

"And the sound of a trumpet, and the voice of words; which *voice* they that heard entreated that the word should not be spoken to them any more:" Vs. 19

Follow the path of the King of righteousness and peace (7:2, 17) with those whose faith enabled them to endure.

Why have they not yet been made perfect? 11:40-12:4

How are we to run the race? Vs. 1, 12-15

How are we to look to Jesus? Vs. 2, 15

What is the purpose of chastening? Vs. 5-11

Where had Moses led the people? Vs. 18-21

What was their response? Vs. 19-20

🕮 DAY 160

READ Hebrews 12:22-29

"And this *word*, Yet once more, signifieth the removing of those things that are shaken, as of things that are made, that those things which cannot be shaken may remain." Vs. 27

Describe *Mount Zion, the city* that God has promised those who look to and follow Jesus? Vs. 22-24, 27-29

Meditate much on today's reading.
What is the difference in the *voice of words* in verse 19 and the voice of Jesus who speaks from heaven? Vs.25-27

Have you received the promise from Jesus? Vs. 25-26

What should be your response? Vs. 28

🕮 DAY 161

READ Hebrews 13:1-25

"Remember them which have the rule over you, who have spoken unto you the word of God: whose faith follow, considering the end of *their* conversation." Vs. 7

"And I beseech you, brethren, suffer the word of exhortation: for I have written a letter unto you in few words." Vs. 22

What are the final words of exhortation to the Hebrews? Vs. 1, 2, 3, 4, 5-6, 7, 17

What is the *end of their conversation*? Vs. 8-16

How is *the heart established*? Vs. 9

What is our association with Christ? Vs. 12-15

How are we *sanctified*? Vs. 12

With what result? Vs. 15

How is all this possible? Vs. 20-21

🌺 Thoughts for Week 23

From this past week's readings how would you describe the power of God's word for our salvation?

Through whom are the promises made?

Through whom did God speak, then, and now?

What is the effect?

What is your hope?

At this point how powerful has the word of God been in your life?

WEEK 24
James 1 ~ 2 Peter 3

Week 24

🕮 DAY 162

READ James 1:1-18

"Of his own will begat he us with the word of truth, that we should be a kind of firstfruits of his creatures." Vs. 18

How are we commanded to face trials? Vs. 2 See Philippians 4:4 and 1 Thessalonians 5:16-18

What is the purpose of our trials? Vs. 3-4, 12

What is needful? Vs. 5

How do we receive wisdom? Vs. 5-8 See Hebrews 11:1, 6 and Hebrews 10:38-39

What is the source of our faith? Vs. 17-18
See Ephesians 2:8-9
Compare verse 18 to John 1:12; 3:3-8; John 8:31-36; 1 Peter 1:23-25; 2 Corinthians 5:17; Ezekiel 36:25-26

Where is life and death in us? Vs. 12-16

🕮 DAY 163

READ James 1:19-27

"Wherefore lay apart all filthiness and superfluity of naughtiness, and receive with meekness the engrafted word, which is able to save your souls. But be ye doers of the word, and not hearers only, deceiving your own selves." Vs. 21,22

To what part of the body is God's wisdom applied? Vs. 19, 26

What is the work of *the engrafted word*? Vs. 21
How are we deceived? Vs. 22, 26 Compare verses 13-16

What is the proof that we are begotten of the word of truth? Vs. 22, 25, 27

What assurance does the *priesthood* of Christ give?

What difference has the study of God's word made this week?

What part of your life has been affected?

What affect has God's word had on your faith?

Pray to understand the *truth* from James 1:18---*that we should be a kind of firstfruits of His creatures,* and 1:27---*to keep himself unspotted from the world.*

🕮 DAY 164

READ 1 Peter 1:1-25

"Being born again, not of corruptible seed, but of incorruptible, by the word of God, which liveth and abideth for ever. But the word of the Lord endureth for ever. And this is the word which by the gospel is preached unto you." Vs. 23, 25

Meditate on 2-3 and 23-25.
Consider these first verses and these last verses of 1 Peter 1, the beginning and the end of *the gospel*.
Between is the filling, the work of the *word of God* in us.
Meditate on verses 1-12.
To what is the gospel referred? Vs. 3, 4, 5, 8, 9, 10, 12

Meditate on 13-15. *Wherefore* indicates the result of the gospel in our lives.
What effect does this *lively hope* cause? Vs. 13-17, 2, 22

How *precious* and valuable is this gospel (this *inheritance*)? Vs. 3, 4, 7, 8, 12, 18-19, 23, 25

At what cost do we have this *inheritance*? Vs. 2, 11, 18-19

Where and when will we receive this full *salvation*? Vs. 4, 5, 7, 13

What role does the *Holy Spirit* have in our salvation? Vs. 2, 11, 12, 22
Meditate on verses 3-5, 10, 20

🕮 DAY 165

READ 1 Peter 2:1-25

"As newborn babes, desire the sincere milk of the word, that ye may grow thereby:"
Vs. 2

"And a stone of stumbling, and a rock of offence, *even to them* which stumble at the word, being disobedient: whereunto also they were appointed."
Vs. 8

The word *wherefore* again comes after the truth of the *word of God*. What is the result of being *born again of the word of God*? (1:23-25; 2:1-2)

Meditate on verses 3-8. What is the difference between those who *believe* and those who are *disobedient*?

Compare the *lively stones* to the *living hope* in 1 Peter 1:3 and the *building* in Ephesians 2:19-22.
Compare the *coming* (4) and the *spiritual sacrifices* (5) to Romans 12:1-2; 1 Corinthians 3;16; 6: 19-20; Hebrews 13:13-16 and Revelation 1:5-6.
What is the blessing and purpose of our *election* (1:2)?
Vs. 9

How does Peter *beseech* them? Vs. 11

What is the will of God for us as strangers and pilgrims? Vs. 15

What is *well-doing*? Vs. 11-14, 16-18

Why are we instructed to *endure grief---suffering wrongfully*? Vs. 19-21

What is His example? Vs. 22-23

What is the result of His suffering for you vs. 24-25

🙞 DAY 166

READ 1 Peter 3:1-22

"Likewise, ye wives, *be* in subjection to your own husbands; that, if any obey not the word, they also may without the word be won by the conversation of the wives;" Vs.

Meditate on 1-7. To what does the word *likewise* refer? Vs. 1, 7 (See chapter 2 for the commands of *subjection*.)

What does the word do? Vs. 1, 2, 4, 6

What is the proper fear? Vs. 2, 15

What is the improper fear? Vs. 6, 13, 14

How are we prepared to suffer for righteousness' sake? Vs. 4, 8, 9. 10, 11, 12, 13; 4:1

What should others see? Vs. 2, 5, 6, 7, 8; 4:2

What should they hear? Vs. 10, 15

Why? Vs. 18, 21, 22

🕮 DAY 167

READ 2 Peter 1:1-21

"We have also a more sure word of prophecy; whereunto ye do well that ye take heed, as unto a light that shineth in a dark place, until the day dawn, and the day star arise in your hearts:" Vs. 9

Meditate on verse 1-3. To whom was Peter's letter written?

How had they *obtained like precious faith*? Vs. 1

How was the *grace and peace of their faith to be multiplied*? Vs. 2, 15

How do we receive this *knowledge*? Vs. 3, 20-21

What is the purpose of this *knowledge*? Vs. 3, 8, 10, 11

What was Peter's role in the knowledge of *these things*? Vs. 12-16

What is given through this knowledge? Vs. 4

What is the result of *the divine nature* in us? Vs. 4, 10-11

What are *these things* that we are *diligent* to *add*? Vs. 5, 6, 7 Compare 1 Peter 5:10-12

🕮 DAY 168

READ 2 Peter 3:1-18

"That ye may be mindful of the words which were spoken before by the holy prophets, and of the commandment of us the apostles of the Lord and Saviour:" Vs. 2

"But the heavens and the earth, which are now, by the same word are kept in store, reserved unto fire against the day of judgment and perdition of ungodly men." Vs. 7

What did Peter want to *stir up*? Vs. 1-2

What were they to *know first*? Vs. 3-4

What were *scoffers ignorant of*? Vs. 5-7, 15-16

What happened by *the word of God*? Vs. 5

How did the world *perish*? Vs. 6

How will the *heaven and earth perish*? Vs. 7, 10-12

According to His *promise* (His word) what is our expectation? Vs. 13, 15

What is God's expectation of us? Vs. 9, 11, 12, 14, 18

What is His warning? 17

🌹 Thoughts for Week 24

Recapture in your own words what the Lord has taught you from His Word this week.

WEEK 25
1 John 1 ~ Revelation 5

🕮 DAY 169

READ 1 John 1:1-10'

"That which was from the beginning, which we have heard, which we have seen with our eyes, which we have looked upon, and our hands have handled, of the Word of life;" Vs. 1

"If we say that we have not sinned, we make him a liar, and his word is not in us." Vs. 10

What is the purpose of *the word* in this chapter? Vs. 1, 2, 3, 4, 5, 7, 9 (Compare 1 John 1:1-3 to John 1:1, & 14)

In whose *life* was the word *manifested* and whose *blood cleanses us from all sin*?

What is the relationship between *truth*, *His word*, and *fellowship*? Vs. 6, 8, 10

Compare Jesus' witness of the Father in John 17 to John's witness in 1 John 1:2, 3.

DAY 170

READ 1 John 2:1-11

"But whoso keepeth his word, in him verily is the love of God perfected: hereby know we that we are in him.
"Brethren, I write no new commandment unto you, but an old commandment which ye had from the beginning.
The old commandment is the word which ye have heard from the beginning." Vs. 5, 7

What is this *fellowship*? See 1: 3

How did *Jesus Christ* become our *advocate*? 2:1-2

What is *propitiation*? (See a Concordance)

What is the proof that we *know* the *Father* and the *Son*? 1 John 2:3, 5, 6

What is the relationship between *His word* and *His commandments*? Vs. 3, 5, 7

What work does His word do? Vs. 5, 10

❦ DAY 171

READ 1 John 2:12-29

"I have written unto you, fathers, because ye have known him *that is* from the beginning. I have written unto you, young men, because ye are strong, and the word of God abideth in you, and ye have overcome the wicked one." Vs. 14

Meditate on verses 12-14. How does John address the people? Vs. 12, 13, 14

Why was he *writing* to them? Vs. 12, 13, 14

What is his counsel to them? Vs. 15-17

What is his warning? Vs. 18-23

What is the assurance? Vs. 21

What is the promise? To those who know the truth? Vs. 24, 25

Meditate on 25-29. What does it mean to *abide*? Vs. 27-28   See vs. 17, 25, 29

🕮 DAY 172

READ 1 John 4:21-5:21

"For there are three that bear record in heaven, the Father, the Word, and the Holy Ghost: and these three are one." Vs. 7

What is the proof that we *believe*? Vs. 21, 1-3

What is the power of the new birth? Vs. 4-5

What is the witness of *Jesus Christ* in vs. 6-8.?

Whose *witness* is this? Vs. 9

What is the result of believing? Vs. 10

What is *the record*? Vs. 11-12

What is the promise in John's writing this letter to believers? Vs. 13

What is the confidence that comes with faith? Vs. 14-16

What does the believer *know*? Vs. 18-20

What does he do? Vs. 2

🕮 DAY 173

READ Revelation 1:1-20

"Who bare record of the word of God, and of the testimony of Jesus Christ, and of all things that he saw." Vs. 2

"I John, who also am your brother, and companion in tribulation, and in the kingdom and patience of Jesus Christ, was in the isle that is called Patmos, for the word of God, and for the testimony of Jesus Christ." Vs. 9

In what way does this book come to John? Vs. 1

For what purpose?

What is the blessing to the reader? Vs. 3

What is the greeting? Vs. 4-5

To whom?

How does he speak of those who are *washed from our sins*? Vs. 5-6

What is the picture of Christ's coming? Vs. 7

What does He say of Himself? Vs. 8

Where was John and how did he receive this revelation? Vs. 9-10

What did Jesus say to John? Vs. 11

What did John hear and see? Vs. 10, 12-16

Compare vs. 16 to Hebrews 4:12, John 6:63;12:47-50 and Matthew 10:34

What was John's response? Vs. 17

What did Jesus say to him? Vs. 17-20

What were the *seven candlesticks*? Vs. 12-13, 20

What were the *seven stars*? Vs. 16, 20

Where are these *stars*? Vs. 16

Who are these *angels*? See Romans 10:14-15

🕮 DAY 174

READ Revelation 3:1-13

"I know thy works: behold, I have set before thee an open door, and no man can shut it: for thou hast a little strength, and hast kept my word, and hast not denied my name.

"Because thou hast kept the word of my patience, I also will keep thee from the hour of temptation, which shall come upon all the world, to try them that dwell upon the earth." Vs. 8, 10

What was wrong in the church in Sardis? Vs. 1-2

What were the instructions to the church? Vs. 2-3

What was Christ's authority and power? Vs. 1-3 (See 5:6)

What was the promise to the *few names*? Vs. 4-5

What were their *works before God*? Vs. 4-5

How is Christ described? Vs. 7

How did He speak of the church in Philadelphia? Vs. 8-9; 10

What is His promise to them? Vs. 10

What are His instructions? Vs. 11

What is the promise for those that *overcome*? Vs. 12
Compare 1 John 5:4-5

🕮 DAY 175

READ Revelation 5:12-6:17
"And when he had opened the fifth seal, I saw under the altar the souls of them that were slain for the word of God, and for the testimony which they held:" Vs. 9

Who is *the Lamb*?
What do the *seals* reveal? Vs. 16, 17

Meditate on verses 9-11. Where are the *souls* of the martyrs?

What are their rewards? Vs. 11   Compare to 1:5-6; 2:26 and 5:8-10

Why were these hiding? Vs. 16, 17 (See 2 Corinthians 4:1-7 Hebrews 1:8-14; 9:27-28; 1 Peter 1:2-7; Jude 24-25; 2 Timothy 3:15; Revelation 15:3-4)

How will you stand before *the Lamb* in that day---hiding from His *face* or sharing His glory?

🕮 Thoughts for Week 25

Of how many different ways is the word of God spoken this past week?

How powerful is His word? How effective is it in your own heart and life? What sins do you need to confess?

WEEK 26
Revelation 11 ~ Revelation 20

🕮 DAY 176

READ Revelation 11:15-12:17

"And they overcame him by the blood of the Lamb, and by the word of their testimony; and they loved not their lives unto the death." Vs. 11

Meditate on 11:15-19. Explain in your own words what you see.

In spite of Satan's attempts to *devour* Christ, what happens" Vs. 5

How was he overcome in *heaven*? Vs. 7-9

How did the *brethren* overcome him? Vs. 10-11
(See Luke 9:22-26; Romans 16:20; 2 Timothy 3:8-13)

How will *the remnant* (the church) overcome? Vs. 11, 17
See Ephesians 6:10-18

🕮 DAY 177

READ Revelation 19:1-21

"And he *was* clothed with a vesture dipped in blood: and his name is called **The Word of God**." Vs. 13
Meditate on verses 1-10. What were *much people* saying? Vs. 1-3

What is the triumph? (See also Acts 17:29-31)

What happens to the great *whore*? Compare verse 3 to Isaiah 34:10

What is the celebration? Vs. 6-9 (See Matthew 22:1-14 and 25:1-13; Ephesians 5:25-27; Revelation 21:2, 9-10)

What is the *fine linen*?

Meditate on the *worship* and *praise* that is taking place in these verses.
What did John see in 11-14? (See 1:14 ,2:17 and 19:2; 2 Thessalonians 2:8; Matthew 26:28;1 Peter 1:16-19; Hebrews 13:20-21; Ephesians 1:6-7; 3:14-15; John 1:1-2)

What is the power of **The Word of God** in verses 15 and 21? (See Hebrews 1:3; 4:12-13; John 12:44-50.)

What are the two *suppers*? Vs. 9, 17-18, 21

What happens to *the beast* and *the kings of the earth* and *their armies*? Vs. 19-21
(See 16:6-11; 18:8-9, 18; 20: 10, 15; Matthew 3:11-12.)

MEDITATE ON PSALM 1.
Are you clothed in the *fine linen* of Jesus' *righteousness*? Is He your *KING* and *LORD*?

🕮 DAY 178

READ Revelation 20:1-15

"And I saw thrones, and they sat upon them, and judgment was given unto them: and *I saw* the souls of them that were beheaded for the witness of Jesus, and for the word of God, and which had not worshipped the beast, neither his image, neither had received *his* mark upon their foreheads, or in their hands; and they lived and reigned with Christ a thousand years." Vs. 4

What did John see in verses 1-3?

What is the reward for those who were *beheaded for the witness of Jesus, and for the word of God, and which had not worshipped the beast, neither had received his mark upon their foreheads*? Vs. 4

What is the *second death*? Vs. 5, 14, 15

What is the *first resurrection*? Vs. 5, 6

What is the purpose for *the book of life*? Vs. 15

What happens when *Satan is loosed*? Vs. 7-10

What is the final triumph? Vs. 11 (See 21:1)

Rejoice as you read the conclusion of God's Word in Chapters 21 and 22

🕮 Conclusive Thoughts and Prayer

Pray for the Spirit of Christ to give you understanding of the power of His word to us and in us.

Write in your own words what you have learned from this section of study on God's Word.

From the Author

Nine years after thinking that my life was coming to an end, God is still working to reveal Himself to me. At the age of seventy-nine, the new heart He gave me twenty-six years ago is continually being filled with His grace. It is through the power of His will that He has enabled me to live joyfully as a caregiver for members of our family: my father with cancer, my grandchildren, my mother with dementia, and my husband, who is an amputee with heart disease and diabetes. There is no better life than that of serving the Master by serving others.

We began writing these wonderful things of His kingdom so as to provide a legacy for our grandchildren. From file boxes to computer documents, we have been publishing books since 2016 that will be available to future generations. They are here for anyone who wants to read of how the Lord works in the hearts and lives of His people as He is preparing us to share His eternal glory. Profits from sales of our books are designated for missions and charity.

"For the Lord is good, His mercy is everlasting, and His truth endures to all generations." Psalm 100:5

🕮 FREE EBook
FIRST THINGS That Last FOREVER

Other books by this author

Blog: godsgracegodsglory.com
Facebook: Father and Family Books
Contact: f.rogers@bellsouth.net

Other Books in Series

*****What the Holy BIBLE Says About LIGHT**
What the Holy BIBLE Says About LIFE

Series *Little Books About the Magnitude of God*
(Published*)

*****FIRST THINGS That Last FOREVER**
*****TWO FULL PLATES ~ Learning to be a Caregiver**
*****The Garden of GOD'S WORD~ The Purpose and
Delight of BIBLE STUDY**
*****The LITTLE BOAT
and other Short Stories of GOD'S GRACE**
*****GOD Is Our Goal**
Child Keeping ~ God's Blessing to Parents
Notes on Paul's Letter to the Romans
Legacy of the Seven Psalms + One
God's Grace ~ God's Glory

Other Books
*****Prayers That Bring the House Down**
*****One Month to Live ~ A Father's Last Words**
*****A Broad Review of Andrew Murray's "Humility"**
Waiting is Not a Game ~ Articles of Faith
My Garden and other Poems of GOD'S GRACE

www.ingramcontent.com/pod-product-compliance
Lightning Source LLC
Chambersburg PA
CBHW031353040426
42444CB00005B/268